KT-218-508

ERIC CLAPTON

THE AUTOBIOGRAPHY

Eric Clapton was born in 1945. At the age of eighteen, he joined the Yardbirds and in 1966, he formed Cream with Ginger Baker and Jack Bruce. Blind Faith and Derek and the Dominos followed before Eric embarked on his solo career which has spanned three decades to date. He has produced dozens of bestselling albums selling tens of millions of copies. He is married with three daughters and lives with his family in Surrey. He also has another daughter, Ruth, by a previous relationship.

ERIC CLAPTON

THE AUTOBIOGRAPHY

By Eric Clapton

with Christopher Simon Sykes

arrow books

Published in the United Kingdom by Arrow Books in 2008

·11

Copyright © Eric Clapton, 2007

Eric Clapton has asserted his right under the Copyright, Designs and
Patents Act, 1988 to be identified as the author of this work.

This book is sold subject to the condition that it shall not,
by way of trade or otherwise, be lent, resold, hired out,
or otherwise circulated without the publisher's prior
consent in any form of binding or cover other than that
in which it is published and without a similar condition,
including this condition, being imposed on the
subsequent purchaser

First published in Great Britain in 2007 by
Century

Arrow Books
Random House, 20 Vauxhall Bridge Road,
London SW1V 2SA

www.rbooks.co.uk

Addresses for companies within The Random House Group Limited can be
found at: www.randomhouse.co.uk/offices.htm

The Random House Group Limited Reg. No. 954009

A CIP catalogue record for this book
is available from the British Library

ISBN 9780099505495

The Random House Group Limited supports The Forest Stewardship
Council® (FSC®), the leading international forest-certification organisation.
Our books carrying the FSC label are printed on FSC®-certified paper.
FSC is the only forest-certification scheme supported by the leading
environmental organisations, including Greenpeace. Our
paper procurement policy can be found at
www.randomhouse.co.uk/environment

Printed and bound in Great Britain by Clays Ltd, St Ives plc

This book is dedicated to my
Grandmother Rose Amelia Clapp,
and to my beloved wife Melia, and
my children Ruth, Julie, Ella and Sophie.

Acknowledgements

For their help in producing this book, I would like to thank Christopher Simon Sykes and Richard Steele, and a special thanks to Nici for all her hard work transcribing the manuscript.